Christmas Homilies of Benedict XVI

by
Pope Benedict XVI

All booklets are published thanks to the generous support of the members of the Catholic Truth Society

CATHOLIC TRUTH SOCIETY
PUBLISHERS TO THE HOLY SEE

Contents

The Christ-Child Brings Love and Peace 3

Signs and Symbolism of the Nativity 10

God Came Down from Heaven for Our Good 16

God's Coming Must Be Met With Song 24

The Story of the Shepherds 32

Christ Came to Fulfil the Prophecies
- We Must Rejoice 40

A Feast of the Heart 48

Sources 55

All rights reserved. First published 2012 by The Incorporated Catholic Truth Society, 40-46 Harleyford Road London SE11 5AY Tel: 020 7640 0042 Fax: 020 7640 0046. Copyright © 2012 Libreria Editrice Vaticana.

ISBN 978 1 86082 819 5

Front cover image: *Pope Benedict XVI kneels as he leads the Christmas Mass in St Peter's Basilica at the Vatican on 25th December, 2008* © MAX ROSSI/Reuters/Corbis.

The Christ-Child Brings Love and Peace

The Son of God

"The Lord said to me: You are my son; this day I have begotten you". With these words of the second Psalm, the Church begins the Vigil Mass of Christmas, at which we celebrate the Birth of Jesus Christ our Redeemer in a stable in Bethlehem. This Psalm was once a part of the coronation rite of the kings of Judah. The People of Israel, in virtue of its election, considered itself in a special way a son of God, adopted by God. Just as the king was the personification of the people, his enthronement was experienced as a solemn act of adoption by God, whereby the King was in some way taken up into the very mystery of God. On Bethlehem night, these words, which were really more an expression of hope than a present reality, took on new and unexpected meaning. The Child lying in the manger is truly God's Son. God is not eternal solitude but rather a circle of love and mutual self-giving. He is Father, Son and Holy Spirit.

God has become one of us

But there is more: in Jesus Christ, the Son of God, God himself, God from God, became man. To him the Father says: "You are my son". God's everlasting "today" has come down into the fleeting today of the world and lifted our momentary today into God's eternal today. God is so great that he can become small. God is so powerful that he can make himself vulnerable and come to us as a defenceless child, so that we can love him. God is so good that he can give up his divine splendour and come down to a stable, so that we might find him, so that his goodness might touch us, give itself to us and continue to work through us. This is Christmas: "You are my son, this day I have begotten you". God has become one of us, so that we can be with him and become like him. As a sign, he chose the Child lying in the manger: this is how God is. This is how we come to know him. And on every child shines something of the splendour of that "today", of that closeness of God which we ought to love and to which we must yield - it shines on every child, even on those still unborn.

The light of God

Let us listen to a second phrase from the liturgy of this holy night, one taken from the Book of the Prophet Isaiah: "Upon the people who walked in darkness a great light has shone" (*Is* 9:1). The word "light" pervades the entire liturgy of tonight's Mass. It is found again in the passage drawn from St Paul's letter to Titus: "The grace of God has appeared" (*Ti* 2:11). The expression "has appeared" in the original Greek says the same thing that was expressed in Hebrew by the words "a light has shone": this "apparition" - this "epiphany" - is the breaking of God's light upon a world full of darkness and unsolved problems. The Gospel then relates that the glory of the Lord appeared to the shepherds and "shone around them" (*Lk* 2:9). Wherever God's glory appears, light spreads throughout the world. St John tells us that "God is light and in him is no darkness" (*1 Jn* 1:5). The light is a source of life.

Light, love and life

But first, light means knowledge; it means truth, as contrasted with the darkness of falsehood and ignorance. Light gives us life, it shows us the way. But light, as a source of heat, also means love. Where there is love, light shines forth in the world; where there is hatred, the world remains in darkness. In the stable of Bethlehem there appeared the great light which the world awaits. In that Child lying in the stable, God has shown his glory - the glory of love, which gives itself away, stripping itself of all grandeur in order to guide us along the way of love. The light of Bethlehem has never been extinguished. In every age it has touched men and women, "it has shone around them". Wherever people put their faith in that Child, charity also sprang up - charity towards others, loving concern for the weak and the suffering, the grace of forgiveness. From Bethlehem a stream of light, love and truth spreads through the centuries. If we look to the saints - from Paul and Augustine to Francis and Dominic, from Francis Xavier and Teresa of Avila to Mother Teresa of

Calcutta - we see this flood of goodness, this path of light kindled ever anew by the mystery of Bethlehem, by that God who became a Child. In that Child, God countered the violence of this world with his own goodness. He calls us to follow that Child.

The light in us

The true mystery of Christmas is the inner brightness radiating from this Child. May that inner brightness spread to us, and kindle in our hearts the flame of God's goodness; may all of us, by our love, bring light to the world! Let us keep this light-giving flame, lit in faith, from being extinguished by the cold winds of our time! Let us guard it faithfully and give it to others! On this night, when we look towards Bethlehem, let us pray in a special way for the birthplace of our Redeemer and for the men and women who live and suffer there. We wish to pray for peace in the Holy Land: Look, O Lord, upon this corner of the earth, your Homeland, which is so very dear to you! Let your light shine upon it! Let it know peace!

"Those whom God loves"

The word "peace" brings us to a third key to the liturgy of this holy night. The Child foretold by Isaiah is called "Prince of Peace". His kingdom is said to be one "of endless peace". The shepherds in the Gospel hear the glad tidings: "Glory to God in the highest" and "on earth, peace...". At one time we used to say: "to men of good will". Nowadays we say "to those whom God loves". What does this change mean? Is good will no longer important? We would do better to ask: who are those whom God loves, and why does he love them? Does God have favourites? Does he love only certain people, while abandoning the others to themselves? The Gospel answers these questions by pointing to some particular people whom God loves. There are individuals, like Mary, Joseph, Elizabeth, Zechariah, Simeon and Anna. But there are also two groups of people: the shepherds and the Wise Men from the East, the "Magi".

Watching and waiting

Tonight let us look at the shepherds. What kind of people were they? In the world of their time, shepherds were looked down upon; they were considered untrustworthy and not admitted as witnesses in court. But really, who were they? To be sure, they were not great saints, if by that word we mean people of heroic virtue. They were simple souls. The Gospel sheds light on one feature which later on, in the words of Jesus, would take on particular importance: they were people who were watchful. This was chiefly true in a superficial way: they kept watch over their flocks by night. But it was also true in a deeper way: they were ready to receive God's Word through the Angel's proclamation. Their life was not closed in on itself; their hearts were open. In some way, deep down, they were waiting for something; they were waiting for God. Their watchfulness was a kind of readiness - a readiness to listen and to set out. They were waiting for a light which would show them the way. That is what is important for God. He loves everyone, because everyone is his creature. But some persons have closed their hearts; there is no door by which his love can enter. They think that they do not need God, nor do they want him. Other persons, who, from a moral standpoint, are perhaps no less wretched and sinful, at least experience a certain remorse. They are waiting for God. They realise that they need his goodness, even if they have no clear idea of what this means. Into their expectant hearts God's light can enter, and with it, his peace. God seeks persons who can be vessels and heralds of his peace. Let us pray that he will not find our hearts closed. Let us strive to be active heralds of his peace - in the world of today.

Christ's peace

Among Christians, the word "peace" has taken on a very particular meaning: it has become a word to designate communion in the Eucharist. There Christ's peace is present. In all the places where the Eucharist is celebrated, a great network of peace spreads through the world. The communities gathered around the Eucharist make up a kingdom of peace as wide as the world itself. When we celebrate the Eucharist we find ourselves in Bethlehem, in the "house of bread". Christ gives himself to us and, in doing so, gives us his peace. He gives it to us so that we can carry the light of peace within and give it to others. He gives it to us so that we can become peacemakers and builders of peace in the world. And so we pray: Lord, fulfil your promise! Where there is conflict, give birth to peace! Where there is hatred, make love spring up! Where darkness prevails, let light shine! Make us heralds of your peace! Amen.

Signs and Symbolism of the Nativity

The sign is a child

In the Gospel the message given by the angels to the shepherds during that holy night, a message which the Church now proclaims to us: "To you is born this day in the city of David a Saviour, who is Christ the Lord. And this will be a sign for you: you will find a babe wrapped in swaddling clothes and lying in a manger" (*Lk* 2:11-12). Nothing miraculous, nothing extraordinary, nothing magnificent is given to the shepherds as a sign. All they will see is a child wrapped in swaddling clothes, one who, like all children, needs a mother's care; a child born in a stable, who therefore lies not in a cradle but in a manger. God's sign is the baby in need of help and in poverty. Only in their hearts will the shepherds be able to see that this baby fulfils the promise of the prophet Isaiah, which we heard in the first reading: "For to us a child is born, to us a son is given; and the government will be upon his shoulder" (*Is* 9:5). Exactly the same sign has been given to us. We too are invited by the angel of God, through the message of the Gospel, to set out in our hearts to see the child lying in the manger.

God asks only for our love

God's sign is simplicity. God's sign is the baby. God's sign is that he makes himself small for us. This is how he reigns. He does not come with power and outward splendour. He comes as a baby - defenceless and in need of our help. He does not want to overwhelm us with his strength. He takes away our fear of his greatness. He asks for our love: so he makes himself a child. He wants nothing other from us than our love, through which we spontaneously learn to enter into his feelings, his thoughts and his will - we learn to live with him and to practise with him that humility of renunciation that belongs to the very essence of love. God made himself small so that we could understand him, welcome him, and love him.

He became a child for all children

The Fathers of the Church, in their Greek translation of the Old Testament, found a passage from the prophet Isaiah that Paul also quotes in order to show how God's new ways had already been foretold in the Old Testament. There we read: "God made his Word short, he abbreviated it" (*Is* 10:23; *Rm* 9:28). The Fathers interpreted this in two ways. The Son himself is the Word, the *Logos*; the eternal Word became small - small enough to fit into a manger. He became a child, so that the Word could be grasped by us. In this way God teaches us to love the little ones. In this way he teaches us to love the weak. In this way he teaches us respect for children. The child of Bethlehem directs our gaze towards all children who suffer and are abused in the world, the born and the unborn. Towards children who are placed as soldiers in a violent world; towards children who have to beg; towards children who suffer deprivation and hunger; towards children who are unloved. In all of these it is the Child of Bethlehem who is crying out to us; it is the God who has become small who appeals to us. Let us pray this night that the brightness of God's love may enfold all these children. Let us ask God to help us do our part so that the dignity of children may be respected. May they all experience the light of love, which mankind needs so much more than the material necessities of life.

The Word made simple

And so we come to the second meaning that the Fathers saw in the phrase: "God made his Word short". The Word which God speaks to us in Sacred Scripture had become long in the course of the centuries. It became long and complex, not just for the simple and unlettered, but even more so for those versed in Sacred Scripture, for the experts who evidently became entangled in details and in particular problems, almost to the extent of losing an overall perspective. Jesus "abbreviated" the Word - he showed us once more its deeper simplicity and unity. Everything taught by the Law and the Prophets is summed up - he says - in the command: "You shall love the Lord your God with all your heart, and with all your soul, and with all your mind… You shall love your neighbour as yourself" (*Mt* 22:37-40). This is everything - the whole faith is contained in this one act of love which embraces God and humanity. Yet now further questions arise: how are we to love God with all our mind, when our intellect can barely reach him? How are we to love him with all our heart and soul, when our heart can only catch a glimpse of him from afar, when there are so many contradictions in the world that would hide his face from us?

Christmas gifts

This is where the two ways in which God has "abbreviated" his Word come together. He is no longer distant. He is no longer unknown. He is no longer beyond the reach of our heart. He has become a child for us, and in so doing he has dispelled all doubt. He has become our neighbour, restoring in this way the image of man, whom we often find so hard to love. For us, God has become a gift. He has given himself. He has entered time for us. He who is the Eternal One, above time, he has assumed our time and raised it to himself on high. Christmas has become the Feast of gifts in imitation of God who has given himself to us. Let us allow our heart, our soul and our mind to be touched by this fact! Among the many gifts that we buy and receive, let us not forget the true gift: to give each other something of ourselves, to give each other something of our time, to open our time to God. In this way anxiety disappears, joy is born, and the feast is created. During the festive meals of these days let us remember the Lord's words: "When you give a dinner or a banquet, do not invite those who will invite you in return, but invite those whom no one invites and who are not able to invite you" (cf. *Lk* 14:12-14). This also means: when you give gifts for Christmas, do not give only to those who will give to you in return, but give to those who receive from no one and who cannot give you anything back. This is what God has done: he invites us to his wedding feast, something which we cannot reciprocate, but can only receive with joy. Let us imitate him! Let us love God and, starting from him, let us also love man, so that, starting from man, we can then rediscover God in a new way!

Christ nourishes us

And so, finally, we find yet a third meaning in the saying that the Word became "brief" and "small". The shepherds were told that they would find the child in a manger for animals, who were the rightful occupants of the stable. Reading Isaiah (1:3), the Fathers concluded that beside the manger of Bethlehem there stood an ox and an ass. At the same time they interpreted the text as symbolising the Jews and the pagans - and thus all humanity - who each in their own way have need of a Saviour: the God who became a child. Man, in order to live, needs bread, the fruit of the earth and of his labour. But he does not live by bread alone. He needs nourishment for his soul: he needs meaning that can fill his life. Thus, for the Fathers, the manger of the animals became the symbol of the altar, on which lies the Bread which is Christ himself: the true food for our hearts. Once again we see how he became small: in the humble appearance of the Host, in a small piece of bread, he gives us himself. All this is conveyed by the sign that was given to the shepherds and is given also to us: the child born for us, the child in whom God became small for us.

Prayers

Let us ask the Lord to grant us the grace of looking upon the crib this night with the simplicity of the shepherds, so as to receive the joy with which they returned home (cf. *Lk* 2:20). Let us ask him to give us the humility and the faith with which St Joseph looked upon the child that Mary had conceived by the Holy Spirit. Let us ask the Lord to let us look upon him with that same love with which Mary saw him. And let us pray that in this way the light that the shepherds saw will shine upon us too, and that what the angels sang that night will be accomplished throughout the world: "Glory to God in the highest, and on earth peace among men with whom he is pleased." Amen!

God Came Down from Heaven for Our Good

Mankind was awaiting the coming of God

"The time came for Mary to be delivered. And she gave birth to her first-born son and wrapped him in swaddling clothes, and laid him in a manger, because there was no room for them in the inn" (*Lk* 2:6f.). These words touch our hearts every time we hear them. This was the moment that the angel had foretold at Nazareth: "You will bear a son, and you shall call his name Jesus. He will be great, and will be called the Son of the Most High" (*Lk* 1:31). This was the moment that Israel had been awaiting for centuries, through many dark hours - the moment that all mankind was somehow awaiting, in terms as yet ill-defined: when God would take care of us, when he would step outside his concealment, when the world would be saved and God would renew all things. We can imagine the kind of interior preparation, the kind of love with which Mary approached that hour. The brief phrase: "[She] wrapped him in swaddling clothes" allows us to glimpse something of the holy joy and the silent zeal of that preparation. The swaddling clothes were ready, so that the child could be given a fitting welcome. Yet there is no room at the inn. In some way, mankind is awaiting God, waiting for him to draw near. But when the moment comes, there is no room for him. Man is so preoccupied with himself, he has such urgent need of all the space and all the time for his own things, that nothing remains for others - for his neighbour, for the poor, for God. And the richer men become, the more they fill up all the space by themselves. And the less room there is for others.

(Do we have) Space for God?

St John, in his Gospel, went to the heart of the matter, giving added depth to St Luke's brief account of the situation in Bethlehem: "He came to his own home, and his own people received him not" (*Jn* 1:11). This refers first and foremost to Bethlehem: the Son of David comes to his own city, but has to be born in a stable, because there is no room for him at the inn. Then it refers to Israel: the one who is sent comes among his own, but they do not want him. And truly, it refers to all mankind: he through whom the world was made, the primordial Creator-Word, enters into the world, but he is not listened to, he is not received.

These words refer ultimately to us, to each individual and to society as a whole. Do we have time for our neighbour who is in need of a word from us, from me, or in need of my affection? For the sufferer who is in need of help? For the fugitive or the refugee who is seeking asylum? Do we have time and space for God? Can he enter into our lives? Does he find room in us, or have we occupied all the available space in our thoughts, our actions, our lives for ourselves?

God finds a way to call out to us

Thank God, this negative detail is not the only one, nor the last one that we find in the Gospel. Just as in Luke we encounter the maternal love of Mary and the fidelity of St Joseph, the vigilance of the shepherds and their great joy, just as in Matthew we encounter the visit of the wise men, come from afar, so too John says to us: "To all who received him, he gave power to become children of God" (*Jn* 1:12). There are those who receive him, and thus, beginning with the stable, with the outside, there grows silently the new house, the new city, the new world. The message of Christmas makes us recognise the darkness of a closed world, and thereby no doubt illustrates a reality that we see daily. Yet it also tells us that God does not allow himself to be shut out. He finds a space, even if it means entering through the stable; there are people who see his light and pass it on. Through the word of the Gospel, the angel also speaks to us, and in the sacred liturgy the light of the Redeemer enters our lives. Whether we are shepherds or "wise men" - the light and its message call us to set out, to leave the narrow circle of our desires and interests, to go out to meet the Lord and worship him. We worship him by opening the world to truth, to good, to Christ, to the service of those who are marginalised and in whom he awaits us.

King David and Christ

In some Christmas scenes from the late Middle Ages and the early modern period, the stable is depicted as a crumbling palace. It is still possible to recognise its former splendour, but now it has become a ruin, the walls are falling down - in fact, it has become a stable. Although it lacks any historical basis, this metaphorical interpretation nevertheless expresses something of the truth that is hidden in the mystery of Christmas. David's throne, which had been promised to last for ever, stands empty. Others rule over the Holy Land. Joseph, the descendant of David, is a simple artisan; the palace, in fact, has become a hovel. David himself had begun life as a shepherd. When Samuel sought him out in order to anoint him, it seemed impossible and absurd that a shepherd-boy such as he could become the bearer of the promise of Israel. In the stable of Bethlehem, the very town where it had all begun, the Davidic kingship started again in a new way - in that child wrapped in swaddling clothes and laid in a manger. The new throne from which this David will draw the world to himself is the Cross. The new throne - the Cross - corresponds to the new beginning in the stable. Yet this is exactly how the true Davidic palace, the true kingship is being built. This new palace is so different from what people imagine a palace and royal power ought to be like. It is the community of those who allow themselves to be drawn by Christ's love and so become one body with him, a new humanity. The power that comes from the Cross, the power of self-giving goodness - this is the true kingship. The stable becomes a palace - and setting out from this starting-point, Jesus builds the great new community, whose key-word the angels sing at the hour of his birth: "Glory to God in the highest, and peace on earth to those whom he loves" - those who place their will in his, in this way becoming men of God, new men, a new world.

Christ came to heal the world

Gregory of Nyssa, in his Christmas homilies, developed the same vision setting out from the Christmas message in the Gospel of John: "He pitched his tent among us" (*Jn* 1:14). Gregory applies this passage about the tent to the tent of our body, which has become worn out and weak, exposed everywhere to pain and suffering. And he applies it to the whole universe, torn and disfigured by sin. What would he say if he could see the state of the world today, through the abuse of energy and its selfish and reckless exploitation? Anselm of Canterbury, in an almost prophetic way, once described a vision of what we witness today in a polluted world whose future is at risk: "Everything was as if dead, and had lost its dignity, having been made for the service of those who praise God. The elements of the world were oppressed, they had lost their splendour because of the abuse of those who enslaved them for their idols, for whom they had not been created" (*Patrologia Latina* 158, 955f.). Thus, according to Gregory's vision, the stable in the Christmas message represents the ill-treated world. What Christ rebuilds is no ordinary palace. He came to restore beauty and dignity to creation, to the universe: this is what began at Christmas and makes the angels rejoice. The earth is restored to good order by virtue of the fact that it is opened up to God, it obtains its true light anew, and in the harmony between human will and divine will, in the unification of height and depth, it regains its beauty and dignity. Thus Christmas is a feast of restored creation.

Angels and men

It is in this context that the Fathers interpret the song of the angels on that holy night: it is an expression of joy over the fact that the height and the depth, heaven and earth, are once more united; that man is again united to God. According to the Fathers, part of the angels' Christmas song is the fact that now angels and men can sing together and in this way the beauty of the universe is expressed in the beauty of the song of praise. Liturgical song - still according to the Fathers - possesses its own peculiar dignity through the fact that it is sung together with the celestial choirs. It is the encounter with Jesus Christ that makes us capable of hearing the song of the angels, thus creating the real music that fades away when we lose this singing-with and hearing-with.

We can reach heaven

In the stable at Bethlehem, heaven and earth meet. Heaven has come down to earth. For this reason, a light shines from the stable for all times; for this reason joy is enkindled there; for this reason song is born there. At the end of our Christmas meditation I should like to quote a remarkable passage from St Augustine. Interpreting the invocation in the Lord's Prayer: "Our Father, who art in heaven", he asks: what is this - heaven? And where is heaven? Then comes a surprising response: "…who art in heaven - that means: in the saints and in the just. Yes, the heavens are the highest bodies in the universe, but they are still bodies, which cannot exist except in a given location. Yet if we believe that God is located in the heavens, meaning in the highest parts of the world, then the birds would be more fortunate than we, since they would live closer to God. Yet it is not written: 'The Lord is close to those who dwell on the heights or on the mountains', but rather: 'the Lord is close to the brokenhearted' (*Ps* 34:18[33:19]), an expression which refers to humility. Just as the sinner is called 'Earth', so by contrast the just man can be called 'Heaven'" (*Sermo in monte* II 5, 17). Heaven does not belong to the geography of space, but to the geography of the heart. And the heart of God, during the holy night, stooped down to the stable: the humility of God is heaven. And if we approach this humility, then we touch heaven.

Then the earth too is made new. With the humility of the shepherds, let us set out, during this holy night, towards the Child in the stable! Let us touch God's humility, God's heart! Then his joy will touch us and will make the world more radiant. Amen.

God's Coming Must Be Met With Song

God looks upon us with love

"Who is like the Lord our God, who is seated on high, who looks far down upon the heavens and the earth?" This is what Israel sings in one of the Psalms (113 [112], 5ff.), praising God's grandeur as well as his loving closeness to humanity. God dwells on high, yet he stoops down to us… God is infinitely great, and far, far above us. This is our first experience of him. The distance seems infinite. The Creator of the universe, the one who guides all things, is very far from us: or so he seems at the beginning. But then comes the surprising realisation: The One who has no equal, who "is seated on high", looks down upon us. He stoops down. He sees us, and he sees me. God's looking down is much more than simply seeing from above. God's looking is active. The fact that he sees me, that he looks at me, transforms me and the world around me. The Psalm tells us this in the following verse: "He raises the poor from the dust…" In looking down, he raises me up, he takes me gently by the hand and helps me - me! - to rise from depths towards the heights. "God stoops down". This is a prophetic word. That night in Bethlehem, it took on a completely new meaning. God's stooping down became real in a way previously inconceivable. He stoops down - he himself comes down as a child to the lowly stable, the symbol of all humanity's neediness and forsakenness. God truly comes down. He becomes a child and puts himself in the state of complete dependence typical of a newborn child. The Creator who holds all things in his hands, on whom we all depend, makes himself small and in need of human love. God is in the stable.

The cloud of God's glory

In the Old Testament the Temple was considered almost as God's footstool; the sacred ark was the place in which he was mysteriously present in the midst of men and women. Above the Temple, hidden, stood the cloud of God's glory. Now it stands above the stable. God is in the cloud of the poverty of a homeless child: an impenetrable cloud, and yet - a cloud of glory! How, indeed, could his love for humanity, his solicitude for us, have appeared greater and more pure? The cloud of hiddenness, the cloud of the poverty of a child totally in need of love, is at the same time the cloud of glory. For nothing can be more sublime, nothing greater than the love which thus stoops down, descends, becomes dependent. The glory of the true God becomes visible when the eyes of our hearts are opened before the stable of Bethlehem.

We must be watchful

St Luke's account of the Christmas story tells us that God first raised the veil of his hiddenness to people of very lowly status, people who were looked down upon by society at large - to shepherds looking after their flocks in the fields around Bethlehem. Luke tells us that they were "keeping watch". This phrase reminds us of a central theme of Jesus's message, which insistently bids us to keep watch, even to the Agony in the Garden - the command to stay awake, to recognise the Lord's coming, and to be prepared. Here too the expression seems to imply more than simply being physically awake during the night hour. The shepherds were truly "watchful" people, with a lively sense of God and of his closeness. They were waiting for God, and were not resigned to his apparent remoteness from their everyday lives. To a watchful heart, the news of great joy can be proclaimed: for you this night the Saviour is born. Only a watchful heart is able to believe the message. Only a watchful heart can instil the courage to set out to find God in the form of a baby in a stable. Let us now ask the Lord to help us, too, to become a "watchful" people.

The song of the angels

St Luke tells us, moreover, that the shepherds themselves were "surrounded" by the glory of God, by the cloud of light. They found themselves caught up in the glory that shone around them. Enveloped by the holy cloud, they heard the angels' song of praise: "Glory to God in the highest heavens and peace on earth to people of his good will". And who are these people of his good will if not the poor, the watchful, the expectant, those who hope in God's goodness and seek him, looking to him from afar?

The Fathers of the Church offer a remarkable commentary on the song that the angels sang to greet the Redeemer. Until that moment - the Fathers say - the angels had known God in the grandeur of the universe, in the reason and the beauty of the cosmos that come from him and are a reflection of him. They had heard, so to speak, creation's silent song of praise and had transformed it into celestial music. But now something new had happened, something that astounded them. The One of whom the universe speaks, the God who sustains all things and bears them in his hands - he himself had entered into human history, he had become someone who acts and suffers within history. From the joyful amazement that this unimaginable event called forth, from God's new and further way of making himself known - say the Fathers - a new song was born, one verse of which the Christmas Gospel has preserved for us: "Glory to God in the highest heavens and peace to his people on earth".

The glory of God

We might say that, following the structure of Hebrew poetry, the two halves of this double verse say essentially the same thing, but from a different perspective. God's glory is in the highest heavens, but his high state is now found in the stable - what was lowly has now become sublime.

God's glory is on the earth, it is the glory of humility and love. And even more: the glory of God is peace. Wherever he is, there is peace. He is present wherever human beings do not attempt, apart from him, and even violently, to turn earth into heaven. He is with those of watchful hearts; with the humble and those who meet him at the level of his own "height", the height of humility and love. To these people he gives his peace, so that through them, peace can enter this world.

The medieval theologian William of Saint Thierry once said that God - from the time of Adam - saw that his grandeur provoked resistance in man, that we felt limited in our own being and threatened in our freedom. Therefore God chose a new way. He became a child. He made himself dependent and weak, in need of our love. Now - this God who has become a child says to us - you can no longer fear me, you can only love me.

The children who suffer

With these thoughts, we draw near this night to the Child of Bethlehem - to the God who for our sake chose to become a child. In every child we see something of the Child of Bethlehem. Every child asks for our love. This night, then, let us think especially of those children who are denied the love of their parents. Let us think of those street children who do not have the blessing of a family home, of those children who are brutally exploited as soldiers and made instruments of violence, instead of messengers of reconciliation and peace. Let us think of those children who are victims of the industry of pornography and every other appalling form of abuse, and thus are traumatised in the depths of their soul. The Child of Bethlehem summons us once again to do everything in our power to put an end to the suffering of these children; to do everything possible to make the light of Bethlehem touch the heart of every man and woman. Only through the conversion of hearts, only through a change in the depths of our hearts can the cause of all this evil be overcome, only thus can the power of the evil one be defeated. Only if people change will the world change; and in order to change, people need the light that comes from God, the light which so unexpectedly entered into our night.

Prayers for Bethlehem

And speaking of the Child of Bethlehem, let us think also of the place named Bethlehem, of the land in which Jesus lived, and which he loved so deeply. And let us pray that peace will be established there, that hatred and violence will cease. Let us pray for mutual understanding, that hearts will be opened, so that borders can be opened. Let us pray that peace will descend there, the peace of which the angels sang that night.

Christmas trees sing praise

In Psalm 96 [95], Israel, and the Church, praises God's grandeur manifested in creation. All creatures are called to join in this song of praise, and so the Psalm also contains the invitation: "Let all the trees of the wood sing for joy before the Lord, for he comes" (v. 12ff.). The Church reads this Psalm as a prophecy and also as a task. The coming of God to Bethlehem took place in silence. Only the shepherds keeping watch were, for a moment, surrounded by the light-filled radiance of his presence and could listen to something of that new song, born of the wonder and joy of the angels at God's coming. This silent coming of God's glory continues throughout the centuries. Wherever there is faith, wherever his word is proclaimed and heard, there God gathers people together and gives himself to them in his Body; he makes them his Body. God "comes". And in this way our hearts are awakened. The new song of the angels becomes the song of all those who, throughout the centuries, sing ever anew of God's coming as a child - and rejoice deep in their hearts. And the trees of the wood go out to him and exult. The tree in St Peter's Square speaks of him, it wants to reflect his splendour and to say: Yes, he has come, and the trees of the wood acclaim him. The trees in the cities and in our homes should be something more than a festive custom: they point to the One who is the reason for our joy - the God who comes, the God who for our sake became a child. In the end, this song of praise, at the deepest level, speaks of him who is the very tree of new-found life. Through faith in him we receive life. In the Sacrament of the Eucharist he gives himself to us - he gives us a life that reaches into eternity. At this hour we join in creation's song of praise, and our praise is at the same time a prayer: Yes, Lord, help us to see something of the splendour of your glory. And grant peace on earth. Make us men and women of your peace. Amen.

The Story of the Shepherds

Christ is announced to the shepherds

"A child is born for us, a son is given to us" (*Is* 9:5). What Isaiah prophesied as he gazed into the future from afar, consoling Israel amid its trials and its darkness, is now proclaimed to the shepherds as a present reality by the Angel, from whom a cloud of light streams forth: "To you is born this day in the city of David a Saviour, who is Christ the Lord" (*Lk* 2:11). The Lord is here. From this moment, God is truly "God with us". No longer is he the distant God who can in some way be perceived from afar, in creation and in our own consciousness. He has entered the world. He is close to us. The words of the risen Christ to his followers are addressed also to us: "Lo, I am with you always, to the close of the age" (*Mt* 28:20). For you the Saviour is born: through the Gospel and those who proclaim it, God now reminds us of the message that the Angel announced to the shepherds. It is a message that cannot leave us indifferent. If it is true, it changes everything. If it is true, it also affects me. Like the shepherds, then, I too must say: Come on, I want to go to Bethlehem to see the Word that has occurred there. The story of the shepherds is included in the Gospel for a reason. They show us the right way to respond to the message that we too have received. What is it that these first witnesses of God's incarnation have to tell us?

We must be awake (to hear God)

The first thing we are told about the shepherds is that they were on watch - they could hear the message precisely because they were awake. We must be awake, so that we can hear the message. We must become truly vigilant people. What does this mean? The principal difference between someone dreaming and someone awake is that the dreamer is in a world of his own. His "self" is locked into this dreamworld that is his alone and does not connect him with others. To wake up means to leave that private world of one's own and to enter the common reality, the truth that alone can unite all people. Conflict and lack of reconciliation in the world stem from the fact that we are locked into our own interests and opinions, into our own little private world. Selfishness, both individual and collective, makes us prisoners of our interests and our desires that stand against the truth and separate us from one another. Awake, the Gospel tells us. Step outside, so as to enter the great communal truth, the communion of the one God. To awake, then, means to develop a receptivity for God: for the silent promptings with which he chooses to guide us; for the many indications of his presence.

Some cannot find him

There are people who describe themselves as "religiously tone deaf". The gift of a capacity to perceive God seems as if it is withheld from some. And indeed - our way of thinking and acting, the mentality of today's world, the whole range of our experience is inclined to deaden our receptivity for God, to make us "tone deaf" towards him. And yet in every soul, the desire for God, the capacity to encounter him, is present, whether in a hidden way or overtly. In order to arrive at this vigilance, this awakening to what is essential, we should pray for ourselves and for others, for those who appear "tone deaf" and yet in whom there is a keen desire for God to manifest himself. The great theologian Origen said this: "If I had the grace to see as Paul saw, I could even now (during the Liturgy) contemplate a great host of angels" (cf. in *Lk* 23:9). And indeed, in the sacred liturgy, we are surrounded by the angels of God and the saints. The Lord himself is present in our midst. Lord, open the eyes of our hearts, so that we may become vigilant and clear-sighted, in this way bringing you close to others as well!

"They made haste"

Let us return to the Christmas Gospel. It tells us that after listening to the Angel's message, the shepherds said one to another: "'Let us go over to Bethlehem' ... they went at once" (*Lk* 2:15f.). "They made haste" is literally what the Greek text says. What had been announced to them was so important that they had to go immediately. In fact, what had been said to them was utterly out of the ordinary. It changed the world. The Saviour is born. The long-awaited Son of David has come into the world in his own city. What could be more important? No doubt they were partly driven by curiosity, but first and foremost it was their excitement at the wonderful news that had been conveyed to them, of all people, to the little ones, to the seemingly unimportant. They made haste - they went at once. In our daily life, it is not like that. For most people, the things of God are not given priority, they do not impose themselves on us directly. And so the great majority of us tend to postpone them. First we do what seems urgent here and now. In the list of priorities God is often more or less at the end. We can always deal with that later, we tend to think.

God must come first

The Gospel tells us: God is the highest priority. If anything in our life deserves haste without delay, then, it is God's work alone. The Rule of St Benedict contains this teaching: "Place nothing at all before the work of God (i.e. the divine office)". For monks, the Liturgy is the first priority. Everything else comes later. In its essence, though, this saying applies to everyone. God is important, by far the most important thing in our lives. The shepherds teach us this priority. From them we should learn not to be crushed by all the pressing matters in our daily lives. From them we should learn the inner freedom to put other tasks in second place - however important they may be - so as to make our way towards God, to allow him into our lives and into our time. Time given to God and, in his name, to our neighbour is never time lost. It is the time when we are most truly alive, when we live our humanity to the full.

Some are close, some are far

Some commentators point out that the shepherds, the simple souls, were the first to come to Jesus in the manger and to encounter the Redeemer of the world. The wise men from the East, representing those with social standing and fame, arrived much later. The commentators go on to say: This is quite natural. The shepherds lived nearby. They only needed to "come over" (cf. *Lk* 2:15), as we do when we go to visit our neighbours. The wise men, however, lived far away. They had to undertake a long and arduous journey in order to arrive in Bethlehem. And they needed guidance and direction. Today too there are simple and lowly souls who live very close to the Lord. They are, so to speak, his neighbours and they can easily go to see him. But most of us in the world today live far from Jesus Christ, the incarnate God who came to dwell amongst us. We live our lives by philosophies, amid worldly affairs and occupations that totally absorb us and are a great distance from the manger.

God calls out to all of us

In all kinds of ways, God has to prod us and reach out to us again and again, so that we can manage to escape from the muddle of our thoughts and activities and discover the way that leads to him. But a path exists for all of us. The Lord provides everyone with tailor-made signals. He calls each one of us, so that we too can say: "Come on, 'let us go over' to Bethlehem - to the God who has come to meet us." Yes indeed, God has set out towards us. Left to ourselves we could not reach him. The path is too much for our strength. But God has come down. He comes towards us. He has travelled the longer part of the journey. Now he invites us: come and see how much I love you. Come and see that I am here. *Transeamus usque Bethlehem*, the Latin Bible says. Let us go there! Let us surpass ourselves! Let us journey towards God in all sorts of ways: along our interior path towards him, but also along very concrete paths - the Liturgy of the Church, the service of our neighbour, in whom Christ awaits us.

"This will be a sign"

Let us once again listen directly to the Gospel. The shepherds tell one another the reason why they are setting off: "Let us see this thing that has happened." Literally the Greek text says: "Let us see this Word that has occurred there." Yes indeed, such is the radical newness of this night: the Word can be seen. For it has become flesh. The

God of whom no image may be made - because any image would only diminish, or rather distort him - this God has himself become visible in the One who is his true image, as St Paul puts it (cf. *2 Co* 4:4; *Col* 1:15). In the figure of Jesus Christ, in the whole of his life and ministry, in his dying and rising, we can see the Word of God and hence the mystery of the living God himself. This is what God is like. The Angel had said to the shepherds: "This will be a sign for you: you will find a babe wrapped in swaddling clothes and lying in a manger" (*Lk* 2:12; cf. 2:16). God's sign, the sign given to the shepherds and to us, is not an astonishing miracle. God's sign is his humility. God's sign is that he makes himself small; he becomes a child; he lets us touch him and he asks for our love. How we would prefer a different sign, an imposing, irresistible sign of God's power and greatness! But his sign summons us to faith and love, and thus it gives us hope: this is what God is like. He has power, he is Goodness itself.

Christ comes to change us

He invites us to become like him. Yes indeed, we become like God if we allow ourselves to be shaped by this sign; if we ourselves learn humility and hence true greatness; if we renounce violence and use only the weapons of truth and love. Origen, taking up one of John the Baptist's sayings, saw the essence of paganism expressed in the symbol of stones: paganism is a lack of feeling, it means a heart of stone that is incapable of loving and perceiving God's love. Origen says of the pagans: "Lacking feeling and reason, they are transformed into stones and wood" (in *Lk* 22:9). Christ, though, wishes to give us a heart of flesh. When we see him, the God who became a child, our hearts are opened. In the Liturgy of the holy night, God comes to us as man, so that we might become truly human. Let us listen once again to Origen: "Indeed, what use would it be to you that Christ once came in the flesh if he did not enter your soul? Let us pray that he may come to us each day, that we may be able to say: I live, yet it is no longer I that live, but Christ lives in me (*Ga* 2:20)" (in *Lk* 22:3).

Yes indeed, that is what we should pray for on this holy night. Lord Jesus Christ, born in Bethlehem, come to us! Enter within me, within my soul. Transform me. Renew me. Change me, change us all from stone and wood into living people, in whom your love is made present and the world is transformed. Amen.

Christ Came to Fulfil the Prophecies - We Must Rejoice

The king is chosen by God

"You are my son, this day I have begotten you" - with this passage from Psalm 2 the Church begins the liturgy of this holy night. She knows that this passage originally formed part of the coronation rite of the kings of Israel. The king, who in himself is a man like others, becomes the "Son of God" through being called and installed in his office. It is a kind of adoption by God, a decisive act by which he grants a new existence to this man, drawing him into his own being. The reading from the prophet Isaiah that we have just heard presents the same process even more clearly in a situation of hardship and danger for Israel: "To us a child is born, to us a son is given. The government will be upon his shoulder" (*Is* 9:6). Installation in the office of king is like a second birth. As one newly born through God's personal choice, as a child born of God, the king embodies hope. On his shoulders the future rests. He is the bearer of the promise of peace.

The king is a child

On that night in Bethlehem this prophetic saying came true in a way that would still have been unimaginable at the time of Isaiah. Yes indeed, now it really is a child on whose shoulders government is laid. In him the new kingship appears that God establishes in the world. This child is truly born of God. It is God's eternal Word that unites humanity with divinity. To this child belong those titles of honour which Isaiah's coronation song attributes to him: Wonderful Counsellor, Mighty God, Everlasting Father, Prince of Peace (*Is* 9:6). Yes, this king does not need counsellors drawn from the wise of this world. He bears in himself God's wisdom and God's counsel. In the weakness of infancy, he is the mighty God and he shows us God's own might in contrast to the self-asserting powers of this world.

The child fulfils the prophecy

Truly, the words of Israel's coronation rite were only ever rites of hope which looked ahead to a distant future that God would bestow. None of the kings who were greeted in this way lived up to the sublime content of these words. In all of them, those words about divine sonship, about installation into the heritage of the peoples, about making the ends of the earth their possession (*Ps* 2:8) were only pointers towards what was to come - as it were signposts of hope indicating a future that at that moment was still beyond comprehension. Thus the fulfilment of the prophecy, which began that night in Bethlehem, is both infinitely greater and in worldly terms smaller than the prophecy itself might lead one to imagine. It is greater in the sense that this child is truly the Son of God, truly "God from God, light from light, begotten not made, of one being with the Father". The infinite distance between God and man is overcome. God has not only bent down, as we read in the Psalms; he has truly "come down", he has come into the world, he has become one of us, in order to draw all of us to himself. This child is truly Emmanuel - God-with-us. His kingdom truly stretches to the ends of the earth. He has truly built islands of peace in the world-encompassing breadth of the holy Eucharist. Wherever it is celebrated, an island of peace arises, of God's own peace. This child has ignited the light of goodness in men and has given them strength to overcome the tyranny of might. This child builds his kingdom in every generation from within, from the heart.

The prophecy is a promise

But at the same time it is true that the "rod of his oppressor" is not yet broken, the boots of warriors continue to tramp and the "garment rolled in blood" (*Is* 9:4f.) still remains. So part of this night is simply joy at God's closeness. We are grateful that God gives himself into our hands as a child, begging as it were for our love, implanting his peace in our hearts. But this joy is also a prayer: Lord, make your promise come fully true. Break the rods of the oppressors. Burn the tramping boots. Let the time of the garments rolled in blood come to an end. Fulfil the prophecy that "of peace there will be no end" (*Is* 9:7). We thank you for your goodness, but we also ask you to show forth your power. Establish the dominion of your truth and your love in the world - the "kingdom of righteousness, love and peace".

First-born

"Mary gave birth to her first-born son" (*Lk* 2:7). In this sentence St Luke recounts quite soberly the great event to which the prophecies from Israel's history had pointed. Luke calls the child the "first-born". In the language which developed within the sacred Scripture of the Old Covenant, "first-born" does not mean the first of a series of children. The word "first-born" is a title of honour, quite independently of whether other brothers and sisters follow or not. So Israel is designated by God in the Book of Exodus (4:22) as "my first-born Son", and this expresses Israel's election, its singular dignity, the particular love of God the Father. The early Church knew that in Jesus this saying had acquired a new depth, that the promises made to Israel were summed up in him. Thus the Letter to the Hebrews calls Jesus "the first-born", simply in order to designate him as the Son sent into the world by God (cf. 1:5-7) after the ground had been prepared by Old

Testament prophecy. The first-born belongs to God in a special way - and therefore he had to be handed over to God in a special way - as in many religions - and he had to be ransomed through a vicarious sacrifice, as St Luke recounts in the episode of the Presentation in the Temple. The first-born belongs to God in a special way, and is as it were destined for sacrifice. In Jesus' sacrifice on the Cross this destiny of the first-born is fulfilled in a unique way. In his person he brings humanity before God and unites man with God in such a way that God becomes all in all.

Christ creates brotherhood

St Paul amplified and deepened the idea of Jesus as firstborn in the Letters to the Colossians and to the Ephesians: Jesus, we read in these letters, is the first-born of all creation - the true prototype of man, according to which God formed the human creature. Man can be the image of God because Jesus is both God and man, the true image of God and of man. Furthermore, as these letters tell us, he is the first-born from the dead. In the resurrection he has broken down the wall of death for all of us. He has opened up to man the dimension of eternal life in fellowship with God. Finally, it is said to us that he is the first-born of many brothers. Yes indeed, now he really is the first of a series of brothers and sisters: the first, that is, who opens up for us the possibility of communing with God. He creates true brotherhood - not the kind defiled by sin as in the case of Cain and Abel, or Romulus and Remus, but the new brotherhood in which we are God's own family. This new family of God begins at the moment when Mary wraps her first-born in swaddling clothes and lays him in a manger. Let us pray to him: Lord Jesus, who wanted to be born as the first of many brothers and sisters, grant us the grace of true brotherhood. Help us to become like you. Help us to recognise your face in others who need our assistance, in those who are suffering or forsaken, in all people, and help us to live together with you as brothers and sisters, so as to become one family, your family.

God gives joy

At the end of the Christmas Gospel, we are told that a great heavenly host of angels praised God and said: "Glory to God in the highest and on earth peace among men with whom he is pleased!" (*Lk* 2:14). The Church, in the *Gloria*, has extended this song of praise, which the angels sang in response to the event of the holy night, into a hymn of joy at God's glory - "we praise you for your glory". We praise you for the beauty, for the greatness, for your goodness, which becomes visible to us this night. The appearing of beauty, of the beautiful, makes us happy without our having to ask what use it can serve. God's glory, from which all beauty derives, causes us to break out in astonishment and joy. Anyone who catches a glimpse of God experiences joy, and on this night we see something of his light. But the angels' message on that holy night also spoke of men: "Peace among men with whom he is pleased".

He loves us so we may love

The Latin translation of the angels' song that we use in the liturgy, taken from St Jerome, is slightly different: "peace to men of good will". The expression "men of good will" has become an important part of the Church's vocabulary in recent decades. But which is the correct translation? We must read both texts together; only in this way do we truly understand the angels' song. It would be a false interpretation to see this exclusively as the action of God, as if he had not called man to a free response of love. But it would be equally mistaken to adopt a moralising interpretation as if man were so to speak able to redeem himself by his good will. Both elements belong together: grace and freedom, God's prior love for us, without which we could not love him, and the response that he awaits from us, the response that he asks for so palpably through the birth of his Son. We cannot divide up into independent entities the interplay of grace and freedom, or the interplay of call and response. The two are inseparably woven together. So this part of the angels' message is both promise and call at the same time. God has anticipated us with the gift of his Son. God anticipates us again and again in unexpected ways. He does not cease to search for us, to raise us up as often as we might need. He does not abandon the lost sheep in the wilderness into which it had strayed. God does not allow himself to be confounded by our sin. Again and again he begins afresh with us. But he is still waiting for us to join him in love. He loves us, so that we too may become people who love, so that there may be peace on earth.

Praise God with singing

St Luke does not say that the angels sang. He states quite soberly: the heavenly host praised God and said: "Glory to God in the highest" (*Lk* 2:13f.). But men have always known that the speech of angels is different from human speech, and that above all on this night of joyful proclamation it was in song that they extolled God's heavenly glory. So this angelic song has been recognised from the earliest days as music proceeding from God, indeed, as an invitation to join in the singing with hearts filled with joy at the fact that we are loved by God. *Cantare amantis est*, says St Augustine: singing belongs to one who loves. Thus, down the centuries, the angels' song has again and again become a song of love and joy, a song of those who love. At this hour, full of thankfulness, we join in the singing of all the centuries, singing that unites heaven and earth, angels and men. Yes, indeed, we praise you for your glory. We praise you for your love. Grant that we may join with you in love more and more and thus become people of peace. Amen.

A Feast of the Heart

God has appeared

The reading from St Paul's Letter to Titus begins solemnly with the word "*apparuit*", which then comes back again in the reading at the Dawn Mass: *apparuit* - "there has appeared". This is a programmatic word, by which the Church seeks to express synthetically the essence of Christmas. Formerly, people had spoken of God and formed human images of him in all sorts of different ways. God himself had spoken in many and various ways to mankind (cf. *Heb* 1:1 - Mass during the Day). But now something new has happened: he has appeared. He has revealed himself. He has emerged from the inaccessible light in which he dwells. He himself has come into our midst. This was the great joy of Christmas for the early Church: God has appeared. No longer is he merely an idea, no longer do we have to form a picture of him on the basis of mere words. He has "appeared".

Good and evil

But now we ask: How has he appeared? Who is he in reality? The reading at the Dawn Mass goes on to say: "the kindness and love of God our Saviour for mankind were revealed" (*Ti* 3:4). For the people of pre-Christian times, whose response to the terrors and contradictions of the world was to fear that God himself might not be good either, that he too might well be cruel and arbitrary, this was a real "epiphany", the great light that has appeared to us: God is pure goodness. Today too, people who are no longer able to recognise God through faith are asking whether the ultimate power that underpins and sustains the world is truly good, or whether evil is just as powerful and primordial as the good and the beautiful which we encounter in radiant moments in our world. "The kindness and love of God our Saviour for mankind were revealed": this is the new, consoling certainty that is granted to us at Christmas.

The God-child

In all three Christmas Masses, the liturgy quotes a passage from the Prophet Isaiah, which describes the epiphany that took place at Christmas in greater detail: "A child is born for us, a son given to us and dominion is laid on his shoulders; and this is the name they give him: Wonder-Counsellor, Mighty-God, Eternal-Father, Prince-of-Peace. Wide is his dominion in a peace that has no end" (*Is* 9:5f.). Whether the prophet had a particular child in mind, born during his own period of history, we do not know. But it seems impossible. This is the only text in the Old Testament in which it is said of a child, of a human being: his name will be Mighty-God, Eternal-Father. We are presented with a vision that extends far beyond the historical moment into the mysterious, into the future. A child, in all its weakness, is Mighty God. A child, in all its neediness and dependence, is Eternal Father. And his peace "has no end". The prophet had previously described the child as "a great light" and had said of the peace he would usher in that the rod of the oppressor, the footgear of battle, every cloak rolled in blood would be burned (*Is* 9:1, 3-4).

Christ brings peace

God has appeared - as a child. It is in this guise that he pits himself against all violence and brings a message that is peace. At this hour, when the world is continually threatened by violence in so many places and in so many different ways, when over and over again there are oppressors' rods and bloodstained cloaks, we cry out to the Lord: O mighty God, you have appeared as a child and you have revealed yourself to us as the One who loves us, the One through whom love will triumph. And you have shown us that we must be peacemakers with you. We love your childish estate, your powerlessness, but we suffer from the continuing presence of violence in the world, and so we also ask you: manifest your power, O God. In this time of ours, in this world of ours, cause the oppressors' rods, the cloaks rolled in blood and the footgear of battle to be burned, so that your peace may triumph in this world of ours.

St Francis of Assisi

Christmas is an epiphany - the appearing of God and of his great light in a child that is born for us. Born in a stable in Bethlehem, not in the palaces of kings. In 1223, when St Francis of Assisi celebrated Christmas in Greccio with an ox and an ass and a manger full of hay, a new dimension of the mystery of Christmas came to light. St Francis of Assisi called Christmas "the feast of feasts" - above all other feasts - and he celebrated it with "unutterable devotion" (*2 Celano* 199; *Fonti Francescane*, 787). He kissed images of the Christ-child with great devotion and he stammered tender words such as children say, so Thomas of Celano tells us (ibid.). For the early Church, the feast of feasts was Easter: in the Resurrection Christ had flung open the doors of death and in so doing had radically changed the world: he had made a place for man in God himself. Now, Francis neither changed nor intended to change this objective order of precedence among the feasts, the inner structure of the faith centred on the Paschal Mystery. And yet through him and the character of his faith, something new took place: Francis discovered Jesus' humanity in an entirely new depth. This human existence of God became most visible to him at the moment when God's Son, born of the Virgin Mary, was wrapped in swaddling clothes and laid in a manger. The Resurrection presupposes the Incarnation. For God's Son to take the form of a child, a truly human child, made a profound impression on the heart of the Saint of Assisi, transforming faith into love. "The kindness and love of God our Saviour for mankind were revealed" - this phrase of St Paul now acquired an entirely new depth. In the child born in the stable at Bethlehem, we can as it were touch and caress God. And so the liturgical year acquired a second focus in a feast that is above all a feast of the heart.

Poverty and humility

This has nothing to do with sentimentality. It is right here, in this new experience of the reality of Jesus' humanity that the great mystery of faith is revealed. Francis loved the child Jesus, because for him it was in this childish estate that God's humility shone forth. God became poor. His Son was born in the poverty of the stable. In the child Jesus, God made himself dependent, in need of human love, he put himself in the position of asking for human love - our love. Today Christmas has become a commercial celebration, whose bright lights hide the mystery of God's humility, which in turn calls us to humility and simplicity. Let us ask the Lord to help us see through the superficial glitter of this season, and to discover behind it the child in the stable in Bethlehem, so as to find true joy and true light.

The Christmas Mass

Francis arranged for Mass to be celebrated on the manger that stood between the ox and the ass (cf. *1 Celano* 85; *Fonti* 469). Later, an altar was built over this manger, so that where animals had once fed on hay, men could now receive the flesh of the spotless lamb, Jesus Christ, for the salvation of soul and body, as Thomas of Celano tells us (cf. *1 Celano* 87; *Fonti* 471). Francis himself, as a deacon, had sung the Christmas Gospel on the holy night in Greccio with resounding voice. Through the friars' radiant Christmas singing, the whole celebration seemed to be a great outburst of joy (*1 Celano* 85, 86; *Fonti* 469, 470). It was the encounter with God's humility that caused this joy - his goodness creates the true feast.

Humility and simplicity

Today, anyone wishing to enter the Church of Jesus' Nativity in Bethlehem will find that the doorway five and a half metres high, through which emperors and caliphs used to enter the building, is now largely walled up. Only a low opening of one and a half metres has remained. The intention was probably to provide the church with better protection from attack, but above all to prevent people from entering God's house on horseback. Anyone wishing to enter the place of Jesus' birth has to bend down. It seems to me that a deeper truth is revealed here, which should touch our hearts on this holy night: if we want to find the

God who appeared as a child, then we must dismount from the high horse of our "enlightened" reason. We must set aside our false certainties, our intellectual pride, which prevents us from recognising God's closeness. We must follow the interior path of St Francis - the path leading to that ultimate outward and inward simplicity which enables the heart to see. We must bend down, spiritually we must as it were go on foot, in order to pass through the portal of faith and encounter the God who is so different from our prejudices and opinions - the God who conceals himself in the humility of a newborn baby. In this spirit let us celebrate the liturgy of the holy night, let us strip away our fixation on what is material, on what can be measured and grasped. Let us allow ourselves to be made simple by the God who reveals himself to the simple of heart. And let us also pray especially at this hour for all who have to celebrate Christmas in poverty, in suffering, as migrants, that a ray of God's kindness may shine upon them, that they - and we - may be touched by the kindness that God chose to bring into the world through the birth of his Son in a stable. Amen.

Sources

This book draws together the homilies of Pope Benedict XVI, which took place at the Vatican Basilica during Midnight Mass from 2005 until 2011:

The Christ-Child Brings Love and Peace:
Saturday, 24th December 2005

Signs and Symbolism of the Nativity:
Sunday, 24th December 2006

God Came Down from Heaven for Our Good:
Monday, 24th December 2007

God's Coming Must Be Met With Song:
Wednesday, 24th December 2008

The Story of the Shepherds:
Thursday, 24th December 2009

Christ Came to Fulfil the Prophecies - We Must Rejoice:
Friday, 24th December 2010

A Feast of the Heart:
Saturday, 24th December 2011

New Companion to
Advent & Christmastide

Advent, Christmas and Epiphany are long established seasons in the Church's calendar, surrounded by many traditions and celebrations. With the reduction of Christmas and New Year, for many, to an extended shopping trip, this companion offers fascinating insight and explanation of the time from December to February each year; how to celebrate these seasons and feasts, and grasp their impact on our daily life.

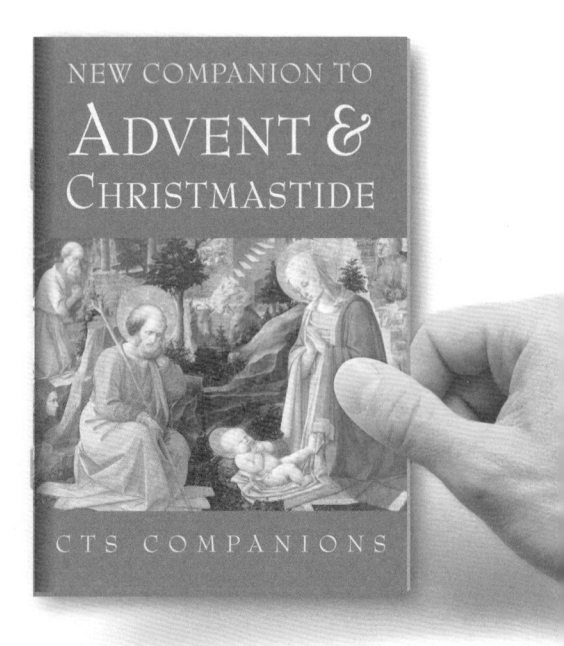

Do 745   ISBN 978 1 86082 402 9